# IS YOUR INTERNAL AUDIT WORLD-CLASS?

## *A MATURITY MODEL FOR INTERNAL AUDIT*

*Norman D. Marks*

Norman Marks, 2019, all rights reserved. ©

*Is your Internal Audit World-Class?*

# Contents

1. Introduction .................................................................................................. 2

2. Maturity Models ........................................................................................... 6

3. How to use the maturity model ................................................................... 9

4. The assessment by the board and top management ................................. 12

5. The end-product ......................................................................................... 16

6. Norman's Maturity Model .......................................................................... 17

About the Author ............................................................................................ 44

# 1. Introduction

*How do you know whether your internal audit function is as effective as it should be?*

*Is it delivering the full value of which it is capable?*

*Is your internal audit world-class?*

Every internal audit function and those responsible for it on the board or audit committee (or equivalent) should know whether it is effective.

The Institute of Internal Auditors (IIA) has a standard, 1310, that requires "both internal and external assessments". External assessments are required at least every five years.

While the IIA is focused, in its Quality Assurance Review, on compliance with its *International Standards for the Professional Practice of Internal Auditing* and *Code of Ethics*, it is also and perhaps more important to determine whether internal audit is delivering on its full potential. If an experienced and imaginative reviewer performs the Quality Assurance Review, it is possible to obtain useful insight on the function's effectiveness and how it can be improved.

There are several ways to assess the quality and effectiveness of the internal audit activity, such as:

- Assess whether the internal audit activity is in compliance with the *International Standards for the Professional Practice of Internal Auditing* and the *Code of Ethics*, from the Institute of Internal Auditors (IIA).

    This only provides assurance of compliance, not necessarily of quality and effectiveness. It might be considered foundational, but doesn't help explore the full potential of internal audit to add value.

    As noted, a Quality Assurance Review can focus only on compliance with IIA Standards and Code of Ethics; it can include compliance with company policies and standards; or it can be more expansive and include an assessment of both efficiency and effectiveness.

- Assess whether the activity achieves the *Core Principles for the Professional Practice of Internal Auditing*[1], also from the IIA.

  Assessing against the Core Principles is an improvement. The three output-focused principles, against which I would assess internal audit, are:

  ❏ Provides risk-based assurance.

  ❏ Is insightful, proactive, and future-focused.

  ❏ Promotes organizational improvement.

  While these are an excellent start, they aren't sufficiently detailed to enable an assessment.

- Obtain an assessment from each of the primary customers of the internal audit activity (i.e., the board and top management) of the value of internal audit services to them and to the organization as a whole.

  Obtaining the assessment of the board and top management is critical. However, they are not always aware of the full potential for valuable assurance and advisory services that can be obtained. They may be content with a moderate rather than fully effective function. A maturity model may help them understand what is possible. I will share more on this later.

  I remember that one of my senior management customers gave me an excellent rating, saying that "you have yet to perform an audit I wouldn't gladly pay for".

  Another customer, the chair of the audit committee of the board, told me that "you help us sleep through the night".

  The first told me that we focused our work on issues that mattered to him and gave him assurance that he could rely on the organization not only to manage risks to enterprise objectives but ensure employee safety, compliance, and optimal performance.

---

[1] I was a member of the IIA Task Force that developed the Principles. They can be found on the IIA's web site.

The second also talked about the issues that mattered to him and the assurance we provided that management would run the company well, addressing the risks that mattered to the board.

- Assess internal audit practices against an acknowledged expert's definition of best practices.

  One expert's view of best practices may not be 'best' for every organization. For example, I have seen evaluations based on factors such as the number of significant findings, the percentage of the audit plan that was completed, and the percentage of findings implemented by management.

    o The number of significant findings is not an indicator of internal audit effectiveness. It is wholly dependent on the effectiveness of management and their commitment to internal control and risk management (and therefore a better assessment rating of management than internal audit). I would argue that significant findings could mean that internal audit was not effective in prior periods in helping management understand and appreciate the value of internal control and the management of risk.

    o Completing a high percentage of the audit plan is often an indicator that the plan was inflexible. This can be an indicator of *ineffectiveness*, as it is essential that the audit plan adapt as business conditions and risk change.

    o While it is comforting when management accepts and implements internal audit recommendations, if the audit team is doing its job well they should be reporting agreed actions rather than recommendations. The danger is that without a constructive dialogue that determines the appropriate action, management will simply go along with internal audit; they might implement a sub-optimal solution.

      For example, my company acquired a wholesale refined oil products terminal that had just been audited from a major company. I was provided a copy of the audit report and saw that internal audit had recommended that the staff in the receiving function not be allowed to see the purchase order when examining what the vendor had delivered. As a result, the possibility was increased that they would record the wrong product or quantity received. It would not be detected until either there was a physical inventory count or production called for the product and found it not to be present in the quantities recorded. The increased risk was small, perhaps, but the system change cost more than $100,000 – a total waste of resources. Management simply went along with the audit recommendation without challenge let alone discussion of its merits.

- Another approach is to utilize all of the above and possible more, including a *maturity model* (also known as a capability maturity model, or CMM).

My preference is to use a combination of assessments by leaders of the organization and a maturity model. I would not use a maturity model alone, as quality should always been seen and assessed through the eyes of the customer.

Additional testing to confirm that individual engagements adhered to policy and standards would be optional.

This book presents a detailed maturity model for internal audit and a list of questions that can be used to help top management and the board make their assessment.

## 2. Maturity Models

Maturity models date back to 1986 when the Software Engineering Institute (SEI) at Carnegie Mellon University developed one for the US government as a "method for assessing the capability of their software contractors[2]."

I like this description[3]:

> CMM can be used to assess an organization against a scale of five process maturity levels. Each level ranks the organization according to its standardization of processes in the subject area being assessed. The subject areas can be as diverse as software engineering, systems engineering, project management, risk management, system acquisition, information technology (IT) services and personnel management.

> CMM was developed by the SEI at Carnegie Mellon University in Pittsburgh. It has been used extensively for avionics software and government projects, in North America, Europe, Asia, Australia, South America, and Africa.

The figure below is a capability model from the US National Aeronautics and Space Administration (NASA)[4]. It uses 5 levels. As you go up each level, the process is considered more 'mature', delivering more value or effectiveness.

*Rest of this page intentionally left blank*

---

[2] Source: SEI, 1993.
[3] Source: Select Business Solutions
[4] Source: Wikimedia Commons

*Is your Internal Audit World-Class?*

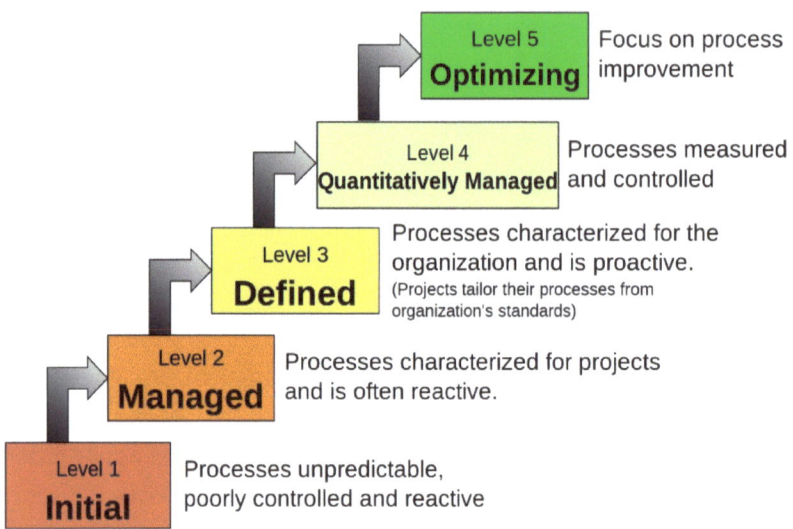

A number of consulting firms and the IIA[5] have developed maturity models for internal audit or for different aspects of internal audit. For example, accounting and other firms[6] have published CMM for the use of data analytics. The figure below is from R!SC[7].

*Rest of this page intentionally left blank*

---

[5] In 2014, IIA Australia shared *Internal Audit Maturity Assessment*, which takes relevant IIA standards and describes performance across five maturity levels. There is also an undated *Internal Audit Process Maturity* document on the IIA web site, and the Internal Audit Foundation updated *Internal Audit Capability Model (IA-CM) for the Public Sector* 2017.
[6] Including Deloitte in 2012 and PwC in 2013.
[7] The illustration is from their 2019 Internal Audit Services Brochure.

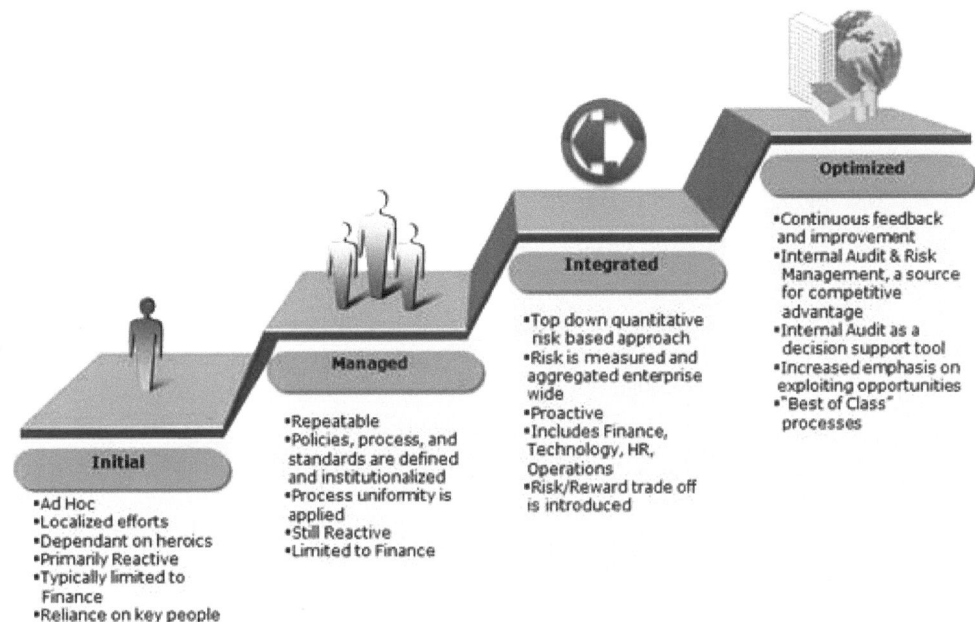

This book shares my own maturity model. It is based on decades of experience leading what has been described as word-class internal auditing departments.

My earlier book, *Auditing that Matters* (2016)[8], provides the detailed thinking behind the maturity model.

Maturity models enable an assessment of an internal audit function that explains where it lies on a maturity curve. Rather than provide a pass/fail assessment of effectiveness, or a vague assessment (such as the 'generally complies' rating used by the IIA's Quality Assessment Review), leadership has a more useful description of where the function is compared to the desired level of maturity.

> "Maturity models provide a way for organizations to determine the current state of the organization as a whole – or any procedure or activity within the organization – as it relates to best practice development. These models can aid in creating development plans and can serve as a tool for internal auditors to use while conducting assessments." IIA Practice Guide, *Selecting, Using, and Creating Maturity Models: A Tool for Assurance and Consulting Engagements* (2013).

---

[8] Available on Amazon

*Is your Internal Audit World-Class?*

## 3. How to use the maturity model

I suggest the following.

1. Review the model suggested below. Adapt as needed for your organization[9]; for example a private company, government agency, or family business may not have an audit committee of the board.

2. Discuss the model and agree with leadership on its use as an assessment tool.

3. Agree with leadership on the *desired* level of maturity, recognizing that this may be aspirational and require time to upgrade existing capabilities and performance.

    A discussion of the merits and values of a more mature function can itself have great value.

4. Agree with leadership how the results of the assessment will be reported. For example, will there be a formal written report and, if so, what form will it take? Will the overall level of maturity be provided, or will only the level for each theme and sub-theme be shared? (See the additional discussions in step 7 and about the end product, below.)

5. Assess current capabilities and performance against the model. Take each row of the model and determine the level of maturity. This will result in multiple assessments, one for each theme and sub-theme.

6. If the maturity level is less than desired, determine and agree on action items.

7. Use judgment to determine how much evidence should be obtained to support the assessment; for example, if this is a self-assessment very little evidence may be required or cost-justified. But if a consultant has been engaged to perform the assessment and report the results to the board, then evidence for each assessment may be appropriate.

---

[9] Use of the model by an organization that has purchased this book to assess its own internal audit function is granted. However, an organization that wants to use it for commercial purposes, such as to support its consulting services, should contact me to obtain approval.

8. Develop the report. There are many ways in which it can be done, including:
    a. A radar or spider chart (as shown in the figure on the next page)
    b. A table that shows, for each theme or sub-theme, the current maturity level. The table on the next page has the same data as the radar chart
    c. A written report that explains and discusses the maturity level of each sub-theme and theme
9. Consider including both the current and the desired maturity level for each theme, together with recommended actions.
10. Discuss the report with leadership, agreeing on action items as appropriate.

As indicated earlier, I do not believe a maturity model is sufficient. It should be accompanied by the assessment of the primary customers of the internal audit function.

The results of the maturity model should be discussed with the board and top management. Helping them understand the features of a world-class function and the great value it can deliver is likely to influence and make more meaningful their assessment.

*Rest of this page intentionally left blank*

*Is your Internal Audit World-Class?*

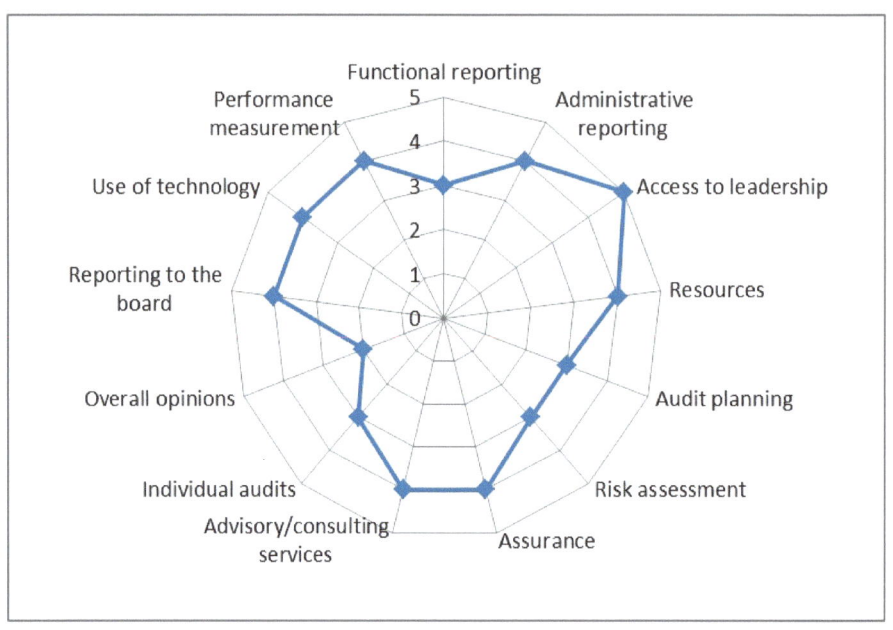

| Theme and sub-theme | Maturity Level |
|---|---|
| Governance | |
| o Functional reporting | 3 |
| o Administrative reporting | 4 |
| o Access to leadership | 5 |
| o Resources | 4 |
| Scope of work | |
| o Audit planning | 3 |
| o Risk assessment | 3 |
| o Assurance | 4 |
| o Advisory/consulting services | 4 |
| Communications | |
| o Individual audits | 3 |
| o Overall opinions | 2 |
| o Reporting to the board | 4 |
| Use of technology | 4 |
| Performance measurement | 4 |

# 4. The assessment by the board and top management

I am a huge believer in the principle that quality and effectiveness should be judged by the customer, not the head of the function.

After all, only the customer knows whether the activity provides him or her with true value. I recall the executive who told me "You have yet to perform an audit I wouldn't gladly pay for".

The primary customer is, for most organizations, the board and its audit committee. Following very closely behind them are the executive management team. Arguably, every manager is a customer and we should seek to add value to them all.

It is important to decide whose opinion will be sought. I recommend:

- Every member of the audit committee of the board
- The chair of the board, if possible
- The CEO and all his or her direct reports
- A number of important customers from among management
- Others as appropriate; I would consider the external auditor or outside counsel

The following set of questions is based on my 2013 article, *How to Assess the Effectiveness of Internal Audit*[10]. They should be modified and expanded to meet specific needs.

1. Do you believe internal audit has provided you with the assurance you need, in a useful way, when you need it, on what matters?

   *Interpretation: 'assurance' is the primary product of internal audit services. It may need to be explained by the interviewer to ensure the customer understands the intent and value of assurance.*

   *This question, supplemented by the following one, focuses on whether the information provided by internal audit is timely, focused on what matters to the board and executive team, and in a form that enables action when necessary.*

---

[10] *Internal Auditor* (online), January 2013

2. Do you have the assurance you need that management has effective and efficient processes and systems to manage the more significant risks to the success of the organization and the achievement of its goals and strategies?

   *Interpretation: the world-class internal audit function provides assurance that the right level of the right risks (which include opportunities) are being taken, so that there is an acceptable likelihood of success – success being measured by the achievement of enterprise objectives.*

3. Has internal audit been sufficiently responsive to changes in risk, ensuring it remains relevant and on point?

   *Interpretation: we live in a dynamic and turbulent world. The best internal audit teams are able to adapt in an agile manner to changes in the business, the conditions around it, and the risks that might affect success. They are flexible in their planning and can re-orient their audit efforts to address the risks that matter today and in the near future, rather than those that existed in the past.*

   *Rather than using a fixed annual plan, world-class functions are constantly modifying their plan in response to changes in business operations, conditions, and related risks and opportunities. They adapt to ensure they are able to deliver assurance and insight that matters, when it matters, and in a form that matters. (Taken from Auditing that Matters.)*

4. Has internal audit been an effective agent for change, improving business efficiency and effectiveness? Have they provided you with useful insights that go beyond the formal report?

   *Interpretation: the best internal audit teams are not satisfied with making recommendations and monitoring to see if they are implemented. Instead, they discuss the issues with management, agree on the facts and the risk they may represent to success, and work together to find the appropriate corrective actions. They are willing not only to work in a consultative manner to help management upgrade processes, but are also able to recognize when the appropriate action is to take the risk.*

   *Management sees internal audit as a trusted partner that is willing to listen as well as speak, working towards agreed assessments of risk and the actions necessary to upgrade performance and achieve success.*

*Internal auditors are also prepared to take a risk themselves and share insights into operations, the personnel, and issues such as culture and morale. While it may not be easy in all cases to obtain persuasive formal evidence, they are open to sharing their thoughts as independent and objective professionals.*

5. Are you satisfied that the cost of internal audit is less than the value of the assurance and consulting services it provides?

    *Interpretation: this is about whether the organization is 'getting its money's worth' from the internal audit function.*

    *There is immense value in having assurance that the processes, systems, organization, and people are capable of doing what is required for success – and that they appear to be performing appropriately when it comes to the more significant risks and opportunities.*

    *There is also huge value in the advice and insight that internal audit can provide that will help the organization continue to upgrade its performance. The question asks whether, in the opinion of internal audit's primary customers, they are getting more value than they are paying in costs.*

6. Are there activities that internal audit should stop performing? Have there been activities you would have preferred not to pay for?

    *Interpretation: this question takes the previous one a step further. It is possible for an internal audit team to deliver against all the points above and yet be performing audit work that is not seen by its primary customers as delivering value.*

7. How can internal audit improve its services to the audit committee, management, and the organization as a whole?

    *Interpretation: this open-ended question should provide an opportunity for a constructive discussion about potential internal audit work that is not currently planned, as well as how the delivery of services could be improved. For example, are there ways to streamline audit reporting to make it easier for customers to not only consume but also to act upon the insights it shares?*

I suggest that the head of internal audit, with input from the CEO and the concurrence of the chair of the audit committee, customize these questions to meet their specific needs.

The questions can form the basis for an annual[11] discussion of performance and how it might be improved. The discussion should not be limited to the questions.

The maturity model can be used to come to a joint understanding of ideal performance by internal audit. Either can be completed first as long as both are included in the assessment.

---

[11] In some organizations, especially where customers are in diverse locations, the assessment of internal audit performance might be continuous, with the CAE or other individual reviewing these questions with management as they visit the area.

## 5. The end-product

The assessment of internal audit performance should not, in my opinion, be a simple pass/fail rating. The goal is to optimize the performance of internal auditing so it provides the assurance, advice, and insight that will help the organization succeed. Therefore, a typical end product would be an agreement by all parties that includes:

- An understanding of whether the desired level of maturity has been achieved
- If not, is the function planning to move up to that level?
- What actions are planned and when will they be completed?
- Is progress acceptable?
- Are additional resources needed and how are they justified?
- How will progress be monitored and reported?

Consider the options for the report discussed in step 7 of *How to use this model*.

## 6. Norman's Maturity Model

The model shared in this book has five levels:
1. Check-the-box
2. Emerging
3. Traditional
4. Integrated
5. World-class

'Check-the-box' is typically found where internal audit is not expected to add much value. It has been established so that the organization can say they have a function and meet compliance requirements, rather than have one they believe will contribute to success.

'Emerging' is primarily about functions that have recently been established. (Some may be 'stuck' at this level for a long time if they are not supported with resources by top management and the board – perhaps because they don't know what they are missing.) They may be unsure of where they need to be. Hopefully, this model can be used to set targets for performance. (Again, details are in *Auditing that Matters*.)

'Traditional' and 'Integrated' are where most internal audit departments lie. While they may be satisfied with current performance, even receiving positive comments from top management and the board, they have yet to achieve world-class, indicated by the highest level of maturity in the model.

The model is built around five themes and sub-themes:

- Governance
    - Functional reporting
    - Administrative reporting
    - Access to leadership
    - Resources

- Scope of work
    - Audit planning
    - Risk assessment
    - Assurance
    - Advisory/consulting services
- Communications
    - Individual audits
    - Overall opinions
    - Reporting to the board
- Use of technology
- Performance measurement

The internal audit function should be assessed for each sub-theme or (for the last two) theme. The assessor may decide to provide an overall assessment if it is clear. However, many functions will have aspects of performance at different levels of maturity. That will indicate where actions may be focused to increase maturity, performance, and the value delivered.

*Rest of this page intentionally left blank*

*Is your Internal Audit World-Class?*

| Theme: Sub-Theme | 1. Check-the box | 2. Emerging | 3. Traditional | 4. Integrated | 5. World-class |
|---|---|---|---|---|---|
| **Governance Structure: Functional reporting** | Reports both functionally and administratively to finance management. All personnel actions regarding the CAE, from hiring/firing to performance assessment and compensation, are determined by management. | Reports functionally to the audit committee. However, the CAE is hired or fired by management, who also set his or her compensation. Management may direct what is included in the audit plan. | Reports functionally to the audit committee. The audit committee chair selects the CAE from among candidates proposed by management. The audit committee approves recommendations from management re compensation and termination of the CAE. | Reports functionally to the audit committee. The audit committee chair selects the CAE from among candidates proposed by management. The audit committee assesses performance and sets CAE compensation with input from management. | Reports functionally to the audit and/or risk committee but also attends the staff meetings of the CEO or CFO. Hiring, performance, appraisals, compensation, and any disciplinary actions are determined by the audit or risk committee with input from management. |

| Theme: Sub-Theme | 1. Check-the box | 2. Emerging | 3. Traditional | 4. Integrated | 5. World-class |
|---|---|---|---|---|---|
| | | | The CAE obtains input from management on the audit plan, but it is approved by the audit committee. | The audit committee decides if the CAE should be disciplined or terminated. | The CAE obtains input from management on the audit plan, but it is approved by the audit committee. |
| | | | | The CAE obtains input from management on the audit plan, but it is approved by the audit committee. | |

*Is your Internal Audit World-Class?*

| Theme: Sub-Theme | 1. Check-the box | 2. Emerging | 3. Traditional | 4. Integrated | 5. World-class |
|---|---|---|---|---|---|
| **Governance Structure:** Administrative reporting | | Reports administratively to the CFO or other direct report to the CEO. | Reports administratively to the CEO, CFO, or other senior executive. | Reports administratively | Reports administratively to the CEO, CFO, or other senior executive.<br><br>In some instances, will report to the lead independent director or the chair of the audit or risk committee. |

21

*Is your Internal Audit World-Class?*

| Theme: Sub-Theme | 1. Check-the box | 2. Emerging | 3. Traditional | 4. Integrated | 5. World-class |
|---|---|---|---|---|---|
| **Governance Structure:** Access to leadership | Has minimal access to either the board or the CEO. May attend and present to the audit committee, but the report is pre-approved by management | Has access to the audit committee but must obtain permission from management.<br><br>Management approves the report by the CAE to the audit committee.<br><br>May have occasional access to the CEO. | Has unrestricted access to the audit committee.<br><br>Has periodic access to the CEO. | Has unrestricted access to the audit committee.<br><br>Has frequent discussions with the CEO. | Has unrestricted access to the audit and other board committees, such as risk and compliance.<br><br>Is consulted by the CEO on major issues. |

*Is your Internal Audit World-Class?*

| Theme: Sub-Theme | 1. Check-the-box | 2. Emerging | 3. Traditional | 4. Integrated | 5. World-class |
|---|---|---|---|---|---|
| **Governance Structure:** *Resources* | Staffing and budget is severely limited. Headcount is often only one or two. Staff are primarily accountants. Staffing may be supplemented by co-sourcing. In some cases, internal audit is outsourced completely. | Staffing and budget are allocated by management based on what they believe is necessary to support a limited audit plan. Staff are primarily accountants. Staffing may be supplemented by co-sourcing. In some cases, internal audit is outsourced completely. | Staffing and budget are based on an audit plan designed to address the more significant locations and their risks. Staff are primarily accountants, supplemented by co-sourcing and guest auditors. In some cases, internal audit is outsourced completely. | Staffing and budget are based on a more expansive audit plan that is enterprise risk-based, but the budget is annual. Staff will have a variety of backgrounds, suitable to address the more significant sources of risk. Co-sourcing and guest auditors are also used. | Staffing and budget are based on what is needed to address the risks that matter to the organization and provide value-added advisory services. The budget may be adjusted as risks and the need for audit services change. The staff is highly experienced, with a variety of backgrounds. They are supplemented by guest auditors and co-sourcing partners. |

*Is your Internal Audit World-Class?*

| Theme: Sub-Theme | 1. Check-the box | 2. Emerging | 3. Traditional | 4. Integrated | 5. World-class |
|---|---|---|---|---|---|
| **Scope of work:** Audit planning | Audit planning is minimal, at best annual. Audits are assigned by management based on their needs. | An annual plan is developed. The greater part of the plan consists of supporting management's assessment of internal control over financial reporting (if mandated). The plan includes audits of select major locations, business units, or locations. | An annual plan is developed. The CAE obtains input from management on the audit plan, but it is approved by the audit committee. The plan is reviewed quarterly and changes may be made with the approval of the audit committee. | An annual plan is developed but it includes a contingency for additional projects to address emerging or changed risks. The plan is reviewed every few months and changes may be made with the approval of the audit committee. | A dynamic and flexible audit plan is maintained. It consists of a list of prioritized audits without a firm timeline, anticipating that the engagements and their timing can change. The focus is on the risks that matter now and in the next twelve months to the enterprise. The plan is updated as risks change, i.e., at the speed of risk. The audit committee allows the CAE to modify the list of prioritized audits, reporting major |

*Is your Internal Audit World-Class?*

| Theme: Sub-Theme | 1. Check-the-box | 2. Emerging | 3. Traditional | 4. Integrated | 5. World-class |
|---|---|---|---|---|---|
| | | Management may direct what is included in the audit plan. | | The CAE obtains input from management on the audit plan, but it is approved by the audit committee. | changes on a quarterly basis. |

| Theme: Sub-Theme | 1. Check-the-box | 2. Emerging | 3. Traditional | 4. Integrated | 5. World-class |
|---|---|---|---|---|---|
| **Scope of work:** Risk assessment | Limited, if any | The plan is risk-based, but only the locations, units, and processes are risk assessed (an 'audit universe' approach). | The plan is based on a risk-prioritized audit universe.<br><br>Few 'full scope' audits are performed. The scope of each audit is limited to the more significant risks to the location, business unit, or process. | The plan is based on a risk-prioritized audit universe, but with some enterprise-level risks included.<br><br>The scope of each audit is limited to the more significant risks to the location, business unit, or process. | The plan is based on a prioritized risk universe, designed to address the risks that matter to the success of the organization and the achievement of its objectives.<br><br>Not only are the risks of the past and today considered, but emphasis is placed on the risks the organization will face over the next period.<br><br>Risks in governance processes are considered in the risk universe. |

*Is your Internal Audit World-Class?*

| Theme: Sub-Theme | 1. Check-the-box | 2. Emerging | 3. Traditional | 4. Integrated | 5. World-class |
|---|---|---|---|---|---|
| **Scope of work: Assurance** | Very limited assurance is provided as few audits are performed and those are directed by management. | A rating system is used to report deficiencies in internal controls for the areas included in scope for individual audits.<br><br>No opinion or assessment is made beyond the rating of deficiencies.<br><br>No formal assessment is made of the overall system of internal control or the management of significant risks. | Assurance is provided on the adequacy of internal controls for the areas included in the scope of individual audits.<br><br>An opinion or assessment is provided in addition to rating the significance of any deficiencies.<br><br>An assessment is made of enterprise risk management based on compliance with policies and | Assurance is provided on the adequacy of internal controls for the areas included in the scope of individual audits.<br><br>An opinion or assessment is provided in addition to rating the significance of any deficiencies.<br><br>An assessment is made of enterprise risk management based on best practices or the achievement of | Assurance is provided on the adequacy of internal controls and the management of risk for the sources of risk included in the scope of individual audits.<br><br>The effect on specific enterprise objectives is included.<br><br>An assessment is made of enterprise risk management, including the management of significant risks to the enterprise, based not only on compliance with policies and standards but whether it provides reasonable assurance that risks are at desired |

| Theme: Sub-Theme | 1. Check-the box | 2. Emerging | 3. Traditional | 4. Integrated | 5. World-class |
|---|---|---|---|---|---|
| | | | standards.<br><br>No formal assessment is made of the overall system of internal control for the management of significant risks to the enterprise. | principles for effective risk management (such as include in ISO 31000:2009).<br><br>A separate assessment is made of made of the overall system of internal control for the management of significant risks to the enterprise. | levels.<br><br>A formal assessment of the overall system of internal control is included in the assessment of the management of significant enterprise risks.<br><br>A combination of assurance and advisory engagements is considered for risks within governance processes. |

*Is your Internal Audit World-Class?*

| Theme: Sub-Theme | 1. Check-the box | 2. Emerging | 3. Traditional | 4. Integrated | 5. World-class |
|---|---|---|---|---|---|
| **Scope of work: Advisory/ consulting services** | Services are provided if directed by management. | Recommendations and (usually) management responses are included in individual audit reports.<br><br>IA reviews and provides advice on internal controls and security on major system implementations. | Internal audit works with management to agree on corrective actions on deficiencies identified in the audits. Recommended actions are reported with management responses.<br><br>IA reviews and provides advice on internal controls and security for major system implementations | Internal audit works with management to agree on corrective actions on deficiencies. Agreed action items are reported and management responses are not necessary.<br><br>IA reviews and provides advice on the management of risk and the adequacy of controls and security for major projects – | Agreed action items are included in each audit reports.<br><br>IA reviews and provides advice on the management of risk and the adequacy of controls and security for major projects – not limited to IT system implementations.<br><br>IA reviews and provides advice on proposed policies and standards.<br><br>IA provides advice and insight to help improve risk and governance processes. |

| Theme: Sub-Theme | 1. Check-the box | 2. Emerging | 3. Traditional | 4. Integrated | 5. World-class |
|---|---|---|---|---|---|
| | | | IA provides advice on new policies and procedures. | not limited to new IT systems.<br><br>IA reviews and provides advice on proposed policies and standards.<br><br>IA provides advice and insight to help improve risk and governance processes. | A combination of assurance and advisory engagements is considered for risks within governance processes.<br><br>The CAE and other members of the IA team provide insight and advice that is not limited to issues identified during an official audit engagement. They are consulted as informed members of the management team. |

*Is your Internal Audit World-Class?*

| Theme: Sub-Theme | 1. Check-the-box | 2. Emerging | 3. Traditional | 4. Integrated | 5. World-class |
|---|---|---|---|---|---|
| **Communications:** Individual audits | A report to management is typically provided on the few audits performed.<br><br>The report includes control deficiencies that are rated high, medium, or low.<br><br>The report may be shared with the audit committee with management permission. | A report is provided to management at the conclusion of every audit.<br><br>The report includes control deficiencies that are rated high, medium, or low.<br><br>A summary of the results of each audit is shared with the audit committee at their meetings. | A report is provided to management at the conclusion of every audit.<br><br>The audit report includes an executive summary of no more than two pages.<br><br>The report includes control deficiencies that are rated high, medium, or low. Management responses are included for each issue. | A report is provided to management at the conclusion of every audit.<br><br>The executive summary is no more than two pages, preferably one.<br><br>The report includes control deficiencies rated high, medium, or low. Agreed action items are included for each issue. | A report is provided to management at the conclusion of every audit.<br><br>The audit report includes an executive summary of no more than two pages, preferably one.<br><br>The report communicates what management and the board need to know about the audit results, not what the auditor wants to say. Unnecessary content (such as background information) is excluded. |

| Theme: Sub-Theme | 1. Check-the box | 2. Emerging | 3. Traditional | 4. Integrated | 5. World-class |
|---|---|---|---|---|---|
| | | An assessment may be included as to whether the controls are adequate or not.<br><br>A copy or summary of each audit report may be sent to the audit committee. | An assessment may be included as to whether the controls are adequate or not.<br><br>The audit report is both fair and balanced, calling out best practices as well as those that need improvement. | An assessment may be included as to whether the controls are adequate or not to address the risks included in the scope of the audit.<br><br>The audit report is both fair and balanced, calling out best practices as well as those that need improvement. | The assessment is of the management of the risks covered by the scope, identifying which enterprise objectives might be affected.<br><br>Agreed action items are included for every issue included in the report.<br><br>The audit report is both fair and balanced, calling out best practices as well as those that need improvement. |

*Is your Internal Audit World-Class?*

| Theme: Sub-Theme | 1. Check-the box | 2. Emerging | 3. Traditional | 4. Integrated | 5. World-class |
|---|---|---|---|---|---|
| | | | A summary of the results of each audit is shared with the audit committee at their meetings. A copy of each audit report may be sent to the audit committee. | On a regular basis, the CAE meets with the CEO and other top executives to discuss the results of audit work, whether there are major business issues, and the status of corrective actions. A summary of the results of each audit is shared with the audit committee. | On a regular basis, the CAE meets with the CEO and other top executives to discuss the results of audit work, whether there are major business issues, and the status of corrective actions. In addition, the CAE and other members of the IA management team discuss with the CEO and other executives the state of the business and the potential for IA to add value. |

| Theme: Sub-Theme | 1. Check-the box | 2. Emerging | 3. Traditional | 4. Integrated | 5. World-class |
|---|---|---|---|---|---|
| | | | | A copy of each audit report may be sent to the audit committee. | Senior executives do not wait for IA to initiate conversations as they know the audit is focused on issues and risks that matter to them.<br><br>A summary of the results of each audit is shared with the audit committee.<br><br>A copy of each audit report may be sent to the audit committee. |

*Is your Internal Audit World-Class?*

| Theme: Sub-Theme | 1. Check-the box | 2. Emerging | 3. Traditional | 4. Integrated | 5. World-class |
|---|---|---|---|---|---|
| **Communications:** Overall opinions | No overall opinion is provided. | No overall opinion is provided. | An assessment is made of enterprise risk management based on compliance with policies and standards.<br><br>No formal assessment is made of the overall system of internal control for the management of significant risks. | An assessment is made of enterprise risk management based on best practices or the achievement of principles for effective risk management (such as include in ISO 31000:2009).<br><br>A separate assessment is made of the overall system of internal control for the management of significant risks to the enterprise. | An assessment is made of enterprise risk management, including the management of significant risks, based not only on compliance with policies and standards but whether it provides reasonable assurance that risks are at desired levels.<br><br>A formal assessment of the overall system of internal control is included in the assessment of the management of significant enterprise risks. |

| Theme: Sub-Theme | 1. Check-the box | 2. Emerging | 3. Traditional | 4. Integrated | 5. World-class |
|---|---|---|---|---|---|
| **Communications:** Reporting to the board | If a report is made at the board or audit committee meeting, it is pre-approved by management. | Provides a report to the audit committee, but it is pre-approved by management. | Provides a report to the audit committee on a quarterly basis that summarizes work performed.<br><br>On an annual basis, the report includes the plan and budget for the upcoming year. | Provides a report to the audit committee on a quarterly basis that summarizes work performed, including any major changes to the approved annual plan.<br><br>On an annual basis, the report includes the plan and budget for the upcoming year. | Provides a report to the audit committee on a quarterly basis that summarizes work performed, including any major changes to the annual plan. In higher performing organizations, an agile and dynamic plan is used, with periodic updates to the audit committee as required.<br><br>On an annual basis, the report includes the plan and budget for the upcoming year. |

*Is your Internal Audit World-Class?*

| Theme: Sub-Theme | 1. Check-the-box | 2. Emerging | 3. Traditional | 4. Integrated | 5. World-class |
|---|---|---|---|---|---|
| | | | | | However, the audit committee accepts the potential for both the plan and the budget to change through the year as business risks change. |

## Is your Internal Audit World-Class?

| Theme: Sub-Theme | 1. Check-the-box | 2. Emerging | 3. Traditional | 4. Integrated | 5. World-class |
|---|---|---|---|---|---|
| **Use of technology** | Basic technology is in place that may include analytics designed for auditors or used by financial analysts. | Basic technology is in place that may include analytics designed for auditors or used by financial analysts. | Basic technology is in place that may include analytics designed for auditors or used by financial analysts.<br><br>Occasional use is made of analytics to support annual as well as individual audit planning. It may also be used for specific testing. | Basic technology is in place that may include analytics designed for auditors or used by financial analysts.<br><br>Frequent use is made of analytics.<br><br>Some continuous auditing is in place, for example for risk monitoring or fraud detection. | All the technology necessary for efficient and effective internal auditing is in place, including mobile analytics and access to the dashboards used by management.<br><br>Larger organizations may use software to assist in staff management, working papers, and related activities. |

*Is your Internal Audit World-Class?*

| Theme: Sub-Theme | 1. Check-the-box | 2. Emerging | 3. Traditional | 4. Integrated | 5. World-class |
|---|---|---|---|---|---|
| | | | | Software is used for audit planning and working papers in larger organizations. | Investments in technology are designed to support an agile audit department. Software and other tools are developed to support the assessment of the management of enterprise risks, not based on which data is available. |

| Theme: Sub-Theme | 1. Check-the box | 2. Emerging | 3. Traditional | 4. Integrated | 5. World-class |
|---|---|---|---|---|---|
| People | The one or two internal auditors may not be very experienced.<br><br>They may or may not have certifications.<br><br>Any IT audit work is typically outsourced. | The CAE is an experienced finance professional but is only in internal audit as a development (or retirement) position. As a result, he or she may not be as objective or assertive. | The CAE is experienced and holds either a CPA, CIA, CISA or equivalent certification.<br><br>The majority of the staff are experienced and certified, but internal audit is seen primarily as a training ground for finance. | The CAE is experienced and holds either a CPA, CIA, CISA or equivalent certification.<br><br>The majority of the staff are experienced and certified. Some have as much as ten years or more internal audit experience.<br><br>The number of junior staff is limited. | The CAE is experienced and holds either a CPA, CIA, CISA or equivalent certification.<br><br>The CAE and several of his direct reports also have experience in line management.<br><br>The majority of the staff are experienced and certified. Some have as much as ten years or more internal audit experience.<br><br>The number of junior staff is limited. |

*Is your Internal Audit World-Class?*

| Theme: Sub-Theme | 1. Check-the box | 2. Emerging | 3. Traditional | 4. Integrated | 5. World-class |
|---|---|---|---|---|---|
| | | The majority of the staff are experienced and certified, but typically don't stay in internal audit more than two or three years. Some staff members are at a junior level and are working towards their certifications. Training is limited. | Some staff members are at a junior level and are working towards their certifications. A minimal number of staff members are IT specialists. Each staff member, including the CAE, receives 3 days or more of annual training. | As many as 10% of the staff are IT specialists. A few members of the staff have other specialist experience and abilities (such as engineers or environmental compliance auditing). Each staff member, including the CAE, receives at least 5 days of annual training. | Staffing includes a variety of specialists, in IT and other critical areas. As many as 25% of the staff are specialists in technology or other critical areas. Each staff member, including the CAE, receives the training necessary for their personal and professional success. |

*Is your Internal Audit World-Class?*

| Theme: Sub-Theme | 1. Check-the box | 2. Emerging | 3. Traditional | 4. Integrated | 5. World-class |
|---|---|---|---|---|---|
| Performance measurement | The performance of IA is based on the subjective assessment of management. | Performance is based on an assessment by management using factors like completion of the audit plan and operating within budget. | Performance is based on an assessment by management using factors like completion of the audit plan, input from the external auditor, and operating within budget.<br><br>The audit committee approves management's assessment with few exceptions. | Performance is based on an assessment by the audit committee of internal audit performance with input from management.<br><br>Factors assessed may include: (a) completion of the audit plan; (b) input from the external auditors; (c) budget compliance; (d) a subjective view of value provided, and | Performance is based on an assessment by the audit committee of internal audit performance with input from management.<br><br>The CAE provides his or her assessment of performance, which is considered by the audit committee in its own assessment.<br><br>The primary factors are: (a) whether the audit committee believes the internal audit function provides the assurance it needs on the management of the more significant risks; |

*Is your Internal Audit World-Class?*

| Theme: Sub-Theme | 1. Check-the box | 2. Emerging | 3. Traditional | 4. Integrated | 5. World-class |
|---|---|---|---|---|---|
| | | | | (e) whether the audit committee believes they have received assurance regarding the more significant risks to the enterprise. | (b) whether the audit committee and management believe internal audit is adding an appropriate level of value through its insight and advice; and<br><br>(c) whether internal audit is proactive, helping to address the risks of today and tomorrow. |
| | | | | | |

# About the Author

**Norman Marks**, CPA, CRMA is a retired chief audit executive and chief risk officer. He also served as a vice president in IT, responsible for information security, contingency planning, network design, the building of two data centers, methodologies, and more.

Norman approaches this topic as an experienced executive, working with top management and the board for enterprise success.

He is a globally-recognized thought leader in the professions of risk management and internal auditing. He is a frequent speaker at conferences and a mentor to individuals and organizations around the world.

Norman has been honored as a Fellow of the *Open Compliance and Ethics Group* and an Honorary Fellow of the *Institute of Risk Management* for his contributions to risk management. He was indicted into the Institute of Internal Auditors *North American Hall of Distinguished Practitioners* in 2018.

He is the author of eight earlier books:

- *Making Business Sense of Technology Risk* (2019)
- *Risk Management in Plain English: A Guide for Executives: Enabling Success through Intelligent and Informed Risk-Taking* (2018)
- *World-Class Risk Management* (2015)
- *World-Class Risk Management for Nonprofits* (co-authored with Melanie L. Herman) (2017)
- *Auditing that Matters (2016)*
- The Institute of Internal Auditors' *Management's Guide to Sarbanes-Oxley Section 404: Maximize Value Within Your Organization*, described as "the best Sarbanes-Oxley 404 guide out there for management" (4$^{th}$ edition, 2017)
- *World-Class Internal Audit: Tales from my Journey* (2014)
- *How Good is your GRC? Twelve Questions to Guide Executives, Boards, and Practitioners* (2014)

Norman is a prolific blogger and social media influencer. You can find him at normanmarks.wordpress.com.

© 2019 Norman Marks All rights reserved

www.ingramcontent.com/pod-product-compliance
Lightning Source LLC
Chambersburg PA
CBHW040411220526
45473CB00004B/1201